The West Highland Way

Jacquetta Megarry

Rucksack Readers

The West Highland Way: a Rucksack Reader

First edition published 2000 by Rucksack Readers, Landrick Lodge, Dunblane, FK15 0HY, UK

Telephone	*01786 824 696 (+44 1786 824 696)*
Fax	*01786 825 090 (+44 1786 825 090)*
Email:	*info@rucsacs.com*
Website	*www.rucsacs.com*

British Library cataloguing in publication data: a catalogue record for this book is available from the British Library.

ISBN 1-898481-09-1

Design by WorkHorse Productions (info@workhorse.co.uk)
Reprographics by Digital Imaging, printed by M&M Press Ltd, Glasgow on waterproof, biodegradable paper
The maps in this book were created for the purpose by Cartographic Consultants © 2000.

Publisher's note

The weather in Scotland is unpredictable year-round. Some parts of the Way may be wet underfoot, other parts are exposed and/or remote from sources of help. You are responsible for your own safety, and for ensuring that your clothing, food and equipment are suited to your needs.

All information was checked prior to publication. However, changes are inevitable: take local advice and look out for waymarkers and other signs eg for temporary diversions.

The West Highland Way: contents

Long Distance Routes in Scotland   4

1 Planning to walk the Way   5
  How long will it take?   6
  Planning your travel   7
  When is the best time of year?   9
  Combining the Way with other activities   9
  The Country Code   10
  Dogs   10
  Camping and low-cost accomodation   11
  What to bring   12
  Notes for novices   13
      Daily mileage   13
      Preparing to walk the Way   14
      The right gear   15
  Packing checklist   18
  Miles and km, feet and metres   20

2 Background information
  2.1   Loch Lomond   21
  2.2   Historical background   26
  2.3   Munros, Corbetts and Grahams   29
  2.4   Habitats and wildlife   31

3 The Way in detail
  3.1   From Glasgow to Milngavie   35
  3.2   Milngavie to Drymen   36
  3.3   Drymen to Rowardennan   39
  3.4   Rowardennan to Crianlarich   43
  3.5   Crianlarich to Inveroran   48
  3.6   Inveroran to Kinlochleven   51
  3.7   Kinlochleven to Fort William   55
  3.8   Fort William and Ben Nevis   58

4 Reference
  Contact details   61
  Acknowledgements   62

  Index   63

  Drop-down map of the Way (1:100,000)   64

Long Distance Routes in Scotland

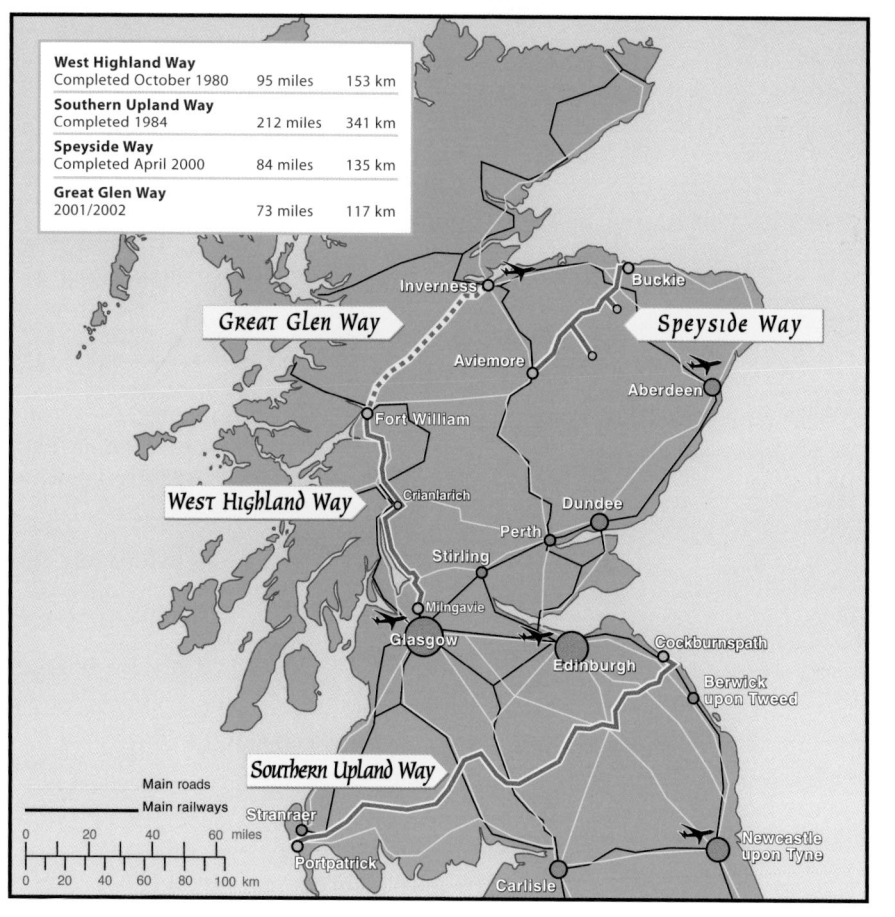

West Highland Way		
Completed October 1980	95 miles	153 km
Southern Upland Way		
Completed 1984	212 miles	341 km
Speyside Way		
Completed April 2000	84 miles	135 km
Great Glen Way		
2001/2002	73 miles	117 km

Long Distance Routes run like threads through Scotland's history. Walk along one and you follow in the footsteps of drovers, pilgrims, soldiers, clansmen, cattle-rustlers and, in places, along the trackbed of disused railways from the 20th century. The map shows Scotland's four official, waymarked Long Distance Routes.

The West Highland Way runs from near Glasgow to Fort William. It was the first, and remains the most popular, of these Long Distance Routes. By 1994, it was already attracting 36,500 people a year, of whom over 60% were long-distance as opposed to day walkers. Over half of these were visitors from outside Scotland.

The West Highland Way is managed jointly by the Loch Lomond and Trossachs Interim Committee and Highland Council, and is substantially funded by Scottish Natural Heritage, the Lottery Sports Fund and European Objectives 1 and 5b.

Planning to walk the Way

The West Highland Way is the first and most famous of Scotland's long-distance routes. The Way begins in Milngavie near Glasgow, its largest city, then goes through Scotland's first proposed national park, along the shores of its largest loch. Loch Lomond forms a water-bridge spanning the lowlands and highlands, with unique geology and wildlife. After 95 miles of superb scenery, the Way ends in Fort William, at the foot of Ben Nevis, Britain's highest mountain.

Some of the walking is straightforward, along tracks, paths and old military roads. Some of it involves scrambling and is boggy underfoot, and other parts can be very exposed and must be taken seriously. If you are not experienced as a walker, read the section 'Notes for novices' (pages 13-18). Well in advance of doing the West Highland Way, you should complete some day walks, to test your feet, gear and fitness.

No such walk should be undertaken casually, because the weather in Scotland is so unpredictable. On any given day, you may experience weather typical of any season, and perhaps of all four. This adds charm and variety to the experience, but also makes it important to have the right equipment (page 15).

This book has been planned in the recommended direction, from south to north, and the drop-down map (back cover) follows this sequence. The gentle lowland gradients will help you to get into your stride before the more exposed and challenging northerly sections. Also, the prevailing wind is south-westerly, so you are more likely to have it at your back.

How long will it take?

You can spread the walk over six, seven or eight days, depending on the time available and the pace you find comfortable. The total of 95 miles excludes the extra distance that you have to walk getting to and from your accommodations. You can also walk the Way in sections, perhaps over several weekends, making use of public transport. Table 1 shows distances along the Way and suggests four ways of dividing up the mileage. Readers who prefer to work in kilometres should refer to page 20.

Table 1	6-day option A	6-day option B	7-day option C	8-day option D
Milngavie				
	12			12
Drymen				
		20	20	
Balmaha				
	15			15
Rowardennan				
		14	14	
Inversnaid				
Inverarnan				14
	20	13	13	
Crianlarich				
Tyndrum				12
		13	13	
Bridge of Orchy				
	16			10
Inveroran				
		13	13	10
Kingshouse				
	18		8	8
Kinlochleven				
	14	22	14	14
Fort William				

Possible overnight stops for 6-, 7- and 8-day walks

You need to plan how to reach the start point and return from the finish, depending on your method and time of travelling from home. Table 2 gives approximate times by various methods, and page 9 suggests how to combine the Way with other activities.

Part 3 describes the Way described in six sections that roughly correspond with the six map panels, but you may not want to walk the whole route in six days. Don't underestimate the time you need: amongst some of Scotland's finest scenery and wildlife, give yourself time 'to stand and stare'. Advice on daily mileage is given on page 13.

Depending on your travelling time to the start and finish of the route, you may prefer Option A (Table 1) that splits the mileage to make shorter start and finish days, allowing some travel time without an extra overnight. Option B is designed for those who intend to overnight at start and finish, allowing full days for walking. Note that both involve demanding schedules on two days out of six. Unless you are both experienced and fit, seven or eight walking days (Options C and D) will put you under less pressure and allow more time for side-trips. Alternatively, use public transport to shorten your walk to fit the holiday time you have available.

Don't leave accommodation to chance: it can be scarce, both out of season and in high summer, and pre-booking is essential. Specialist providers (page 61) can organise it all for you, or you can book for yourself. You need not always stay exactly where your day's walking begins or ends: for example, accommodation at Inveroran is very limited, but a taxi back to Bridge of Orchy would widen your choice. For longer distances, use buses and trains.

Planning your travel

To plan your travel, consult the maps together with the table below, which shows the fastest scheduled times for bus and train (as of early 2000). Car journey times are the fastest likely within speed limits, with no allowance for traffic holdups, and minimal fuel/meal stops. All figures are rough guidelines only: contact details for transport providers are given on page 61. Check travel details carefully in advance, as not all services are daily and winter timetables have fewer services than summer.

Table 2	Miles (approx)	by bus	by train
Glasgow / Fort William	100	3h	3h 45m
Glasgow / Crianlarich	48	1h 30m	1h 50m
Crianlarich / Fort William	52	1h 30m	1h 45m
Edinburgh / Fort William	145	4h	5h
Edinburgh / Glasgow	45	1h	50m
London / Glasgow	400	8h 15m	5h 10m

Distances and fastest journey times between selected places

If you are flying in from outside the UK, renting a car at Glasgow airport may seem attractive. However, you would have to find somewhere reasonably safe to leave the car for a week, and allow time to return to it from the other end of the walk. It may be cheaper, as well as simpler, to use public transport and taxis. Bankell Farm campsite near Milngavie offers car parking for a nightly fee.

If you live locally, you might consider leaving a car at Crianlarich and using the train to reach the start (and return from the finish) of the Way. This would allow you to exchange some clothing and other supplies part way. You could arrange to park it at the B&B or hotel where you are staying, but the arrangement would be entirely at your own risk.

If you have a non-walking driver in your group, he or she can arrange to rendezvous with hikers. The fold-out map (back cover) shows where main roads meet the Way, and also the railway stations. Note that Scottish Citylink operates through buses up the A82 which stop at Luss, Arrochar, Ardlui, Crianlarich, Tyndrum, Bridge of Orchy, Glencoe and Fort William. There is also a local service between Fort William and Kinlochleven via Ballachulish.

> *i*
>
> *Below and throughout, these signpost diagrams show the sequence of places, not their location: for example, you start by walking north from Milngavie.*
>
> *The white numbers show distances in miles; see page 20 for kilometre conversion.*

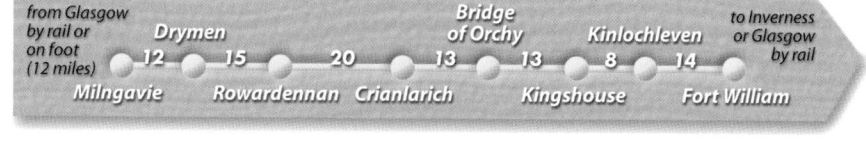

When is the best time of year?

Fortunately for those who have little choice over their holiday dates, there is no *bad* time of year to walk the Way. Be prepared for cold, wet and windy weather at any time and you may be pleasantly surprised. Here are a few factors to think about:

- Winter is less flexible for walkers, because the days are so much shorter: high latitude means that the hours of daylight vary from 6-7 hours in late December to 17-18 in late June.
- Winter restricts your choice of side-trips, which may be open only from April to October.
- Winter hikers are free of pests such as midges and clegs.
- On winter timetables, public transport is less frequent.
- In summer, there will be many more tourists around and heavy pressure on accommodation; however, in winter many B&Bs are closed for the season.

On balance, and if you are free to choose, the ideal months are probably May/June and September/early October. Note that Conic Hill is normally closed for lambing during late April/early May. Also one-week motorbike trials are held annually between Bridge of Orchy and Fort William around the same time: contact official sources (page 61) for firm dates.

Combining the Way with other activities

Many people wish to share their holiday with a partner or friend. If the other person prefers not to walk, you can still rendez-vous easily, especially if one of you drives a car. Many activities combine well with hiking the Way, such as golf, fishing, scenic driving or researching family history. The Tourist Information Centres (page 62) can provide information leaflets on specialist holidays.

For anyone interested in serious hill-climbing or mountaineering, there is enormous scope, mainly north of Rowardennan. Three famous mountains include Ben Nevis (Britain's highest), Ben Lomond (the most southerly Munro) and Buachaille Etive Mor (arguably the most shapely). Please take mountain safety seriously (page 30).

For those that wish to ski, Nevis Range Centre, northeast of Fort William, has Britain's only, and controversial, mountain gondola on the slopes of Aonach Mor. The trip takes 15 minutes to climb to 2150 feet: open daily from Christmas to early November (tel 01397 705 825). Details of Glencoe Ski Centre, south of Kingshouse, are on page 52.

The Country Code

Any long-distance route that attracts many visitors can strain the goodwill of landowners and tenant farmers. A single careless tourist can spoil things for the vast majority of considerate walkers. Please remember that you are a guest on someone else's property. Follow the Country Code.

Be aware that the countryside provides a livelihood for its residents. Lambing takes place from February to May: never disturb pregnant ewes, nor touch young lambs, or they may be 'mis-mothered'.

If you meet cattle on an unfenced section, give them a wide berth: they may resent your presence. Although an attack is very unlikely, take special care not to come between a cow and its calf, and stay alert until you are well clear.

Deer stalking and game shooting take place near the Way at various times of year. These sporting activities contribute to the economy of the area, and do not affect your use of the Way. Please stick closely to the waymarked route.

Dogs

Dogs – even well-behaved ones on leads – are not allowed on certain parts of the West Highland Way. These are shown clearly on the map; where there is a simple dog-friendly bypass, it is shown at the foot of the relevant page in Part 3. There are no obvious alternatives to the sections from north of Inversnaid to Crianlarich, nor Tyndrum to Bridge of Orchy.

The dog prohibitions are part of the agreement with local landowners, and responsible dog-owners will understand the importance of respecting them. There are no dog restrictions north of Bridge of Orchy, but many accommodations do not accept dogs; check carefully before booking.

The Country Code

- ✓ **Respect the life and work of the countryside.**
- ✓ **Guard against all risk of fire.**
- ✓ **Leave gates as you find them, open or carefully closed.**
- ✓ **Keep dogs under strict control.**
- ✓ **Keep to established footpaths, to reduce damage.**
- ✓ **Use gates and stiles to cross fences and walls.**
- ✓ **Leave livestock, crops and machinery alone.**
- ✓ **Take litter home.**
- ✓ **Help to safeguard water supplies.**
- ✓ **Protect wildlife, plants and trees.**
- ✓ **Take care on country roads.**
- ✓ **Avoid making unnecessary noise.**

Camping and other low-cost accommodation

There is a wide range of low-cost accommodation along the Way: the table lists these from south to north. A bothy is a basic roofed stone shelter with a sleeping platform and fireplace. There are bothies on Loch Lomondside at Doune and Rowchoish (map panels 2/3); their use is free of charge.

Bothies	Free campsites	Commercial campsites	Wigwams	Hostels/bunkhouses
		Bankell Farm, Milngavie		
		Gartness		
	Garadhban Forest	Easter Drumquhassle	Easter Drumquhassle	
		Oak Tree Inn, Balmaha		Balmaha
	Milarrochy Bay		Rowardennan	
Rowchoish	Rowardennan	Cashel		
Doune	Inversnaid	Ardlui (for ferry, see page 25)		Crianlarich
		Beinglas Farm	Beinglas Farm	
	Kirkton Farm	Auchtertyre Farm	Auchtertyre Farm	
	Bridge of Orchy	Pinetrees, Tyndrum		Tyndrum, Bridge of Orchy
	Inveroran	Kinlochleven (choice of two)		Kinlochleven
	Kingshouse	Glen Nevis		Glen Nevis

Wild camping is not allowed anywhere on the Way. The free campsites have no facilities, do not allow fires to be lit, and may restrict you to a single night's stay. For more flexibility and luxury, use a commercial campsite: charges vary, but most have toilets and showers, and some have laundries.

Then there are wigwams – timber buildings offering basic facilities, pre-booking advised. There are youth hostels at Rowardennan, Crianlarich and Glen Nevis (see page 62). Finally, there are bunkhouses at Balmaha (Highland Way Hotel annex), Tyndrum (Pinetrees campsite), Bridge of Orchy (hotel annex and station) and Kinlochleven.

Wigwam at Auchtertyre Farm, Strath Fillan

11

What to bring

People vary widely – both in what they need for comfort, and what weight they can readily carry in a rucksack. Before you set limits, decide who is carrying your overnight stuff. If you want to bring more than the bare minimum, book Travel-Lite (page 61) to handle your baggage. It operates (from mid-April to late September) a daily van collecting and delivering luggage at intervals along the Way. This means your luggage has to be ready for collection between 0800 and 1000 daily, and you will need to reach Milngavie (page 35) before 1000 on your first day. Wherever you stay, you will have to carry your luggage from your accommodation or campsite to the Travel-Lite pickup point, so ask about this distance when booking.

If you are camping and on a tight budget, expect to carry heavy weights. This kind of serious backpacking is strictly for the fit and experienced hiker.

If you decide to book B&Bs or guest houses independently, don't assume you will need help with your baggage. Start by reviewing what you need to walk comfortably each day, and if the overnight extras are little more than clean underwear and a toothbrush, consider carrying them rather than relying on baggage handling.

Look through the packing checklist on pages 18-19 before deciding your approach, and plan any important shopping well in advance. Once on the Way, village shops may have limited choice. On some sections, for example Kinlochleven to Fort William (14 miles), there are no refreshments en route, so you must carry everything you need for the day.

Notes for novices

If you've never tackled one before, the idea of a long-distance walk may seem daunting. Some people assume that it's strictly for fitness freaks, that you need years of experience or that you have to spend a fortune on special gear: wrong on all three counts. With careful planning and sensible preparation, any healthy person of any age can complete the West Highland Way and enjoy a special sense of achievement.

Rough terrain near Rob Roy's cave

Daily mileage

It is hard to predict how many miles a day you will manage comfortably. Not only do individuals vary enormously, but also the same person walks at different speeds on different terrain, or if part of a group. Some factors affecting your average speed are:

- group size and fitness
- terrain and gradient
- quality of the surroundings and the weather.

A group travels at the pace of its slowest member, or a little less. Terrain is crucial: through a peat-bog, or on loose gravel, you will walk slowly and tire more quickly. Gradient affects progress, however fit you are, and walking downhill can be surprisingly tiring. In splendid weather you may enjoy lingering, whereas in lashing rain, looking forward to a hot shower, your progress may be astonishing.

A simple rule is this: if you are walking steadily long-distance on the flat, you may average around 2½ miles per hour overall; if you are climbing or the terrain is rough, expect 2 miles per hour or even less. (These figures exclude prolonged stops, but allow for brief pauses to admire the view or take a photo.) On this basis, a 14-mile day may take around 5-6 hours of walking, which many hikers find very comfortable, whereas a tough 20-mile day (eg Rowardennan to Crianlarich) could take 9-11 hours. Many walkers will prefer to split this over two days, as suggested in the seven- and eight-day options.

Preparing to walk the Way

Walking the Way is different from a 'normal' holiday: you will be exercising continuously and carrying your world with you for a week. Give special thought to:

- feet
- weight
- the right gear.

Detailed notes on these are below, but you don't need to spend a lot to get started. The priorities are to buy and break in a decent pair of walking boots well in advance, and buy or borrow a rucksack. Everything else can be acquired gradually, once you're ready to have another go. Don't forget to test everything out on some day walks before you set off.

Feet

Your feet are about to become the most important part of your body. This applies especially if your normal routine involves a lot of sitting down. Unlike after weekend hiking, your feet won't have all week to recover before the next assault. Sore feet can dominate your day, your holiday and your conversation. Don't be a blister bore, or, worse still, drop-out. Tour operators estimate that blisters are responsible for up to 95% of all drop-outs.

Some simple precautions can avoid all this. Your most important purchase is comfortable walking boots (see *The right gear* below). However good the boots, only you can 'break them in', ie let your feet and boots get used to each other. Start by wearing them around the house. Then try a half-day walk, maybe up a small hill, and if all is well test them out on progressively longer and tougher day hikes. If problems surface, take them back to the shop: better socks and insoles may help, and specialists can adjust the fit.

If you are prone to blisters, try rubbing your feet with surgical spirit (rubbing alcohol) daily for a couple of weeks before you set off on holiday. It helps to toughen the skin. Even if you've never had blisters in your life, there's always a first time. So take a pack of adhesive second-skin (see page 18). Even if you don't need it yourself, you may meet someone in agony: there is no cheaper way to make a lifelong friend.

Weight

If you are happy to travel very light, you can carry everything in your day rucksack and stay independent. If you need various luxuries for your holiday, get others to handle your baggage. However, you will still have to handle your overnight bag at the start and finish of your week, so keep its weight manageable. The less clutter you bring, the less effort you will spend on packing and unpacking. Dress among hikers is always informal.

The right gear

Boots

To buy walking boots, ideally go to a specialist outdoor/hiking shop on a weekday. Take your time over the decision: buy in haste, repent at leisure. Good shops will allow you to wear boots indoors and exchange them if they prove uncomfortable: check before you buy, and keep the receipt. Take, borrow or buy suitable socks, and remember that your feet will expand when warm: a common mistake is to buy boots that are too short. Specialist fitters can fix almost anything else about a boot, but if it is too short, they are helpless. Forget your normal shoe size; just focus on how the boot feels.

Try to test downhill walking if there is a practice slope: if your toes press against the end, the boot is too short. Ideally, the boot should have a waterproof, breathable inner layer, but this adds to the cost and may make your feet feel hotter. Don't be sidetracked by boots that seem a bargain, or look smart: the only thing that matters is whether they are comfortable. Some people find a better insole (or footbed) makes a boot feel much softer, so leave room to try this. Also, good walking socks can make a big difference: some people swear by two pairs, a thin liner sock inside a thick outer.

The main choice in boots is between the traditional leather and modern fabric boot. The latter tend to be lighter, and may need less 'breaking in'. Tell the sales people what kind of walking you expect to do, and ask their advice.

Rucksack

The advice below refers to a simple day rucksack; if you are camping and carrying your own gear, you need a much larger, heavy-duty rucksack. Even for daytime use, buy a rucksack that's larger than you think you need: it makes for easier retrieval and packing. Around 35 litres gives plenty of room for spare clothing and water. Don't expect the rucksack to be waterproof: either buy a waterproof cover or liner, or use a bin (garbage) bag. Check that the rucksack

- is comfortable to wear (test it heavily loaded in the shop)
- has a chest strap as well as a waist strap
- is easy to put on and take off
- has side pockets for small items
- has loops for poles (see below)
- is large enough for all you need.

Poles

If you haven't tried using poles yet, borrow one or two to try. Most people find they improve balance, save effort (up to 30%), and reduce knee strain, especially going downhill. They are telescopic: set them longer for downhill, shorter for uphill. Try before you buy: a pair is more efficient, especially on rough, steep terrain, but some people need a hand free for camera, binoculars or dog. However, poles are lightweight and can be stowed on your rucksack loops when not needed.

You will soon discover other uses for poles: pointing, digging mud out of boot soles, brushing brambles aside, testing the depth of flood-water, even self-defence. If you are serious about photography, consider the kind which unscrews at the top to form a camera monopod.

Clothing

The reason for needing special clothing is that your internal temperature varies so much while hiking. This is due to changes in the weather (sun, wind and rain) and in your body's heat production – rapid on an uphill climb, slower when you pause or stop.

To avoid excessive sweating, you may need to shed heat quickly. To avoid chilling, next to your body you need fabrics that 'wick' (draw away) moisture. Avoid cotton (especially denim) as it soaks up moisture (eg sweat, rainwater) and then you become cold.

To control your body temperature, use a layer system. The base layer should ideally be a synthetic 'wicking' fabric, typically polyester or specially treated cotton, eg Ventile. Over that, wear a medium-weight fleece, eg Polartec. The outer layer is a waterproof jacket and trousers; if possible, buy or borrow 'breathable' waterproofs that allow sweat to evaporate. This three-layer combination will keep you warm and dry even in a downpour and high wind. If you are lucky with the weather, the outer two layers weigh little in your rucksack.

Look for flexibility eg trousers whose lower legs unzip to make shorts, and jackets with underarm zips. In addition, pack a warm hat and gloves: never underestimate the Scottish climate.

Water carrier

Few people carry sufficient water, and even fewer keep it handy. You dehydrate quickly when walking, though you may not notice it. Every time you breathe out, you lose moisture, especially when the air is cold. Top up your fluid intake as often as you can, and expect to drink two to four litres per day.

You are advised not to drink casual water without treating it. Purification tablets weigh little, and give you an unlimited safe supply. To override the slight flavour, use neutralising tablets or fruit-flavoured powder. Really strenuous walkers may be interested in isotonic drinks, ie water with added minerals to replace what you lose when sweating a lot. Isotonic powder is expensive, but you can make your own this way: mix 50% fruit juice with 50% water (drinking or treated), then add a pinch of salt and shake.

The cheapest container is a screwtop plastic bottle, worth buying because it's leakproof. However, a water bottle is of little use in the bottom of your rucksack. Try a special plastic water bag or bladder, such as a Platypus. The tube threads through your rucksack strap, so you can take a sip hands-free whenever you feel like it. That way, you drink *before* you get dehydrated.

If you are staying at a B&B, hand in your water holder and your host will normally fill and refrigerate it overnight: just remember to collect it at breakfast. Mark your water carrier with your initials to avoid confusion.

Blister prevention and treatment

What you need is variously sold as Compeed, Moleskin or Second skin. Use it as soon as you feel a blister coming on, or even before, to prevent one. Follow instructions carefully about warming it first and removing the backing paper. Then cover the whole area, letting it bond to the non-blistered skin. About a week later, it will fall off, by which time you will have finished your walk and forgotten the pain.

However, this miraculous stuff is useless unless you carry it in your day rucksack. Nobody develops blisters in the middle of the night.

Packing checklist

The checklist below refers to your daytime needs, and is divided into essential and desirable. Experienced walkers may disagree about what belongs in each category, but novices may appreciate a starting-point. Normally you will be wearing the first two items and carrying the rest in your rucksack.

Essential

- walking boots
- suitable clothing, including good socks
- hat, gloves and waterproofs
- water carrier and plenty of water (or purification tablets)
- food or snacks (depending on distance from next supply point)
- guidebook and/or maps
- blister treatment and first aid kit
- insect repellent: in summer months, expect midges (small biting insects) and/or clegs (horse-flies), notably in still weather
- waterproof rucksack cover or liner eg bin (garbage) bag
- enough cash in pounds sterling for the week

Cash is suggested because credit cards are not always acceptable and cash machines are not common along the Way. Bin bags have many uses, eg storing wet clothing, preventing hypothermia (cut holes for your head and arms).

Desirable

- compass, map, whistle and torch: essential if you are doing any 'serious' side-trips or hiking in winter
- pole(s)
- binoculars: useful for navigation and spotting wildlife
- camera: ideally light and rugged; remember spare batteries and film
- pouch or secure pockets: to keep small items handy but safe
- gaiters: keep trouser legs clean and dry in mud or snow
- toilet tissue (biodegradable)
- weather (sun and wind) protection for eyes and skin
- water purification tablets
- spare socks: changing socks at lunchtime can relieve damp feet
- spare shoes (eg trainers), spare bootlaces
- paper and pen.

If you are camping, you will need much more gear, including tent, groundsheet, sleeping mat and sleeping bag. You may also want a camping stove, cooking utensils and food. If you are carrying everything on your back, you will need to be strong, experienced and well-organised.

Two final, if delicate, issues: first, where should you 'go' if caught short on the Way? The official advice is

- Use public toilets wherever possible.
- If you need to relieve yourself out of doors, pass water well away from streams, paths and bothies.
- Excrement poses health risks, and is unpleasant for others. If you have to go, choose a discreet spot at least 50 yards away from streams, paths and bothies, preferably further. If possible, bury waste in a hole six inches deep; some people carry a trowel for the purpose.

The second is what about mobile phones? You should not rely on one for personal safety: reception may be poor or your battery low. It is unfair to other people to let non-essential mobile chatter disturb their peace and the wildlife. However, if you insist on a mobile phone, as of 2000 the networks with best coverage along the Way are Cellnet and Vodafone; but don't count on having a signal around the northern half of Loch Lomond.

Miles and kilometres, feet and metres

Distances are given mainly in miles, and heights in feet, to suit the habits of most British readers. The diagrams below are to help readers to convert between systems. The quick rule-of-thumb is:

- to convert miles to km, add 50% (and round up a bit)
- to convert feet to metres, divide by three (and round down a bit) where the final correction is less than 10% and does not always matter.

Another way of converting is to use this distance line:

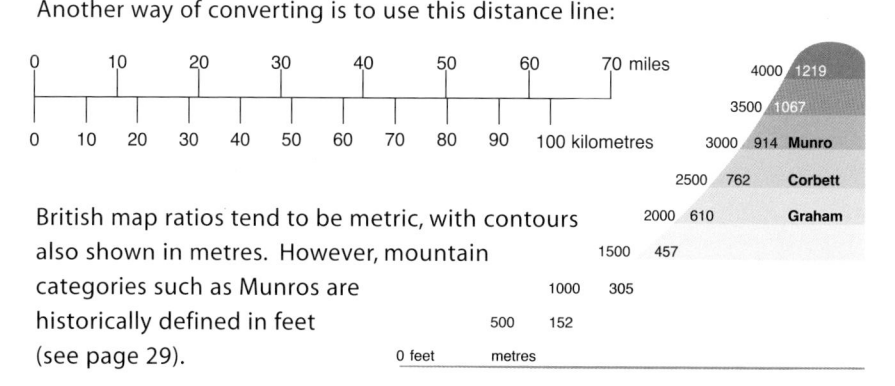

British map ratios tend to be metric, with contours also shown in metres. However, mountain categories such as Munros are historically defined in feet (see page 29).

2.1 Loch Lomond

The southern part of the Way is dominated by Britain's largest body of inland water (by area), and arguably its most beautiful: Loch Lomond. This section lists some general facts, then describes its geology, wildlife, history and communications.

- The loch is 22 miles long and up to 5 miles wide, with an area of $27\frac{1}{2}$ square miles and 38 islands, of which only four are north of Ross Point. The Way follows the eastern lochside for almost 20 miles.

- Its deepest part is near Inversnaid, where it sinks to over 623 feet. The southern loch is generally much shallower, only 40-50 feet south of Inchcailloch. In the extreme winter of 1895, it froze so deeply that thousands of people came to skate and walk on the loch.

- The islands have been the sites of crannogs (see page 24), prisons, churches, graveyards, castles and religious foundations. Most are privately owned, and many are Sites of Special Scientific Interest. Inchcailloch is part of the National Nature Reserve (see page 41).

- The area is rich in plant and bird life: over one quarter of British wild plants have been recorded, as have 200 of Britain's 230 or so native bird species.

- The loch is a major water supply: up to 100 million gallons may be taken from it daily. This would lower its level by just over two inches if not offset by inflow from rivers and rainfall.

- More than 75% of the water draining into the loch comes from the higher, wetter land in the north, drained by the River Falloch system.

Geology

Although joined as a single body of water, there are really two Loch Lomonds: north of Ross Point is a loch 13 miles long but less than a mile wide, with typical highland scenery of high mountains plunging steeply to its deep waters. This northern loch has only four islands, all small and near the shore. Joined to it is the shallow southern loch: 8 or 9 miles long and up to 5 miles wide, it is surrounded by low-lying farming land with rolling hills beyond. Large wooded islands are scattered across it, some still inhabited.

This contrast is no coincidence, since the Highland Boundary Fault passes right through the loch. This divides Scotland's highlands from lowlands, the ancient heat-hardened ('metamorphic') rocks giving way to the younger, more easily eroded sandstones and conglomerates of the south. You can see the line of this fault clearly from Conic Hill (photograph below).

The Fault is, of course, a corridor or zone, rather than a neat thin line. It marks a contrast between highland and lowland that runs through natural and human history in this area.

The basic geology of the area was probably settled by about 350 million years ago. During the ice age, perhaps a million years ago, Loch Lomond was scoured out by the southward flow of the glaciers. Before then, most of the rivers used to drain eastward. The Rivers Falloch and Endrick have probably both changed direction since the Ice Age.

Once the ice retreated, some 10,000 years ago, Loch Lomond emerged in roughly its present shape but as a sea loch, connected with the Firth of Clyde along the Vale of Leven. By about 5,500 years ago, sea level had dropped, leaving it cut off as a freshwater loch. Nowadays it lies only around 26 feet above sea level, rising and falling by up to 10 feet. Look out for evidence of previous high water levels, for example the notice on the boat shed just north of Inversnaid.

From Conic Hill, looking southwest along the line of Inchcailloch and Inchmurrin

Wildlife

The loch supports a rich variety of plants, algae, insects and 18 species of fish, from tiny sticklebacks to coarse fish such as roach, perch and huge pike. A curiosity is the powan (Coregonus), a salmonid fish which occurs only here and in Loch Eck (another former sea loch). Because they feed on plankton, powan are little known to fishermen, although fairly widespread in the loch. River lamprey here are an entirely freshwater species.

On and near the water, you will see common ducks such as mallards and tufted ducks, as well as terns and various gulls which build their nests on the islands. Look out for dippers (good swimmers, despite unwebbed feet) and wagtails (grey and pied), and for fish-eating birds: cormorants and saw-billed ducks such as red-breasted merganser and goosander. Other diving ducks such as goldeneye and pochard are sometimes seen in the quieter northern parts of the loch. In spring you might see visitors such as red-throated and black-throated divers.

Tufted duck

Wildlife that lives along the lochside and on the wetlands near the mouth of the Endrick is described in section 2.4.

The islands make good nesting sites for birds

History

Although humans have probably lived on Loch Lomondside for over 7000 years, the evidence you are likely to see is more recent: early human settlements on *crannogs* and (much later) *cashels*. A crannog is an artificial island dating from the Iron Age (around 2000 years ago); some continued in use well into the middle ages.

People made them by sinking boulders and logs in a shallow area of loch or river until the top rose above the water. Then they built a hut on a timber foundation, sometimes linking it to the shore with a causeway just below the water surface. East of the island of Inchcailloch is 'The Kitchen' crannog, and when the loch is low you can see its causeway. Another good example is in the water just south of Strathcashell Point.

On the Point itself, there is a cashel – a structure dating from early Christian times, enclosed by a dry-stone wall. The remains suggest an enclosure of around 90 feet by 80 feet, with a rectangular building which may have been religious. St Kessog, an Irish monk, built a monastery on Inchtavannach in the sixth century, and his statue is in the church at Luss.

St Kentigerna, another Irish missionary, settled on Inchcailloch, an ideal place to appreciate Loch Lomond's history (page 41). After her death in AD 733-4, a group of nuns continued to live and worship there. In the 13th century, a church was built and dedicated to her. It acted as parish church until 1621, when it fell into decay. Burials continued on Inchcailloch until 1947.

You will see dates from 1623 onward; weathering has eroded the older dates. A table stone marks the grave of Gregor, Chief of Clan MacGregor and uncle of Rob Roy (page 27). Although Gregor died in 1693, his grave stone was later recarved and shows the date as 1623.

Inchcailloch burial ground

Communications

The loch forms a barrier to east-west communications. Apart from the A82 trunk road up the west shore, the only roads are:

- a minor road to Rowardennan from the south
- a single-track road reaching Inversnaid from the east

and the only connection between these two is by walking the Way.

- The West Highland Line railway runs up the west shore from Tarbet northward. Tarbet lies on the narrow neck of land only 100 feet high separating Loch Lomond from the sea in Loch Long. This obstacle was overcome in 1263, when 40 Viking longships from King Haakon's fleet sailed up Loch Long. They were then hauled overland and sailed down Loch Lomond, raiding and burning.

- Nowadays, three ferry services ply in summer (see table below), operated by hotels in Rowardennan, Inversnaid and Ardlui respectively. There are also cruises from Tarbet (01301 702 356).

- To visit Inchcailloch from Balmaha, contact McFarlane's Boatyard (01360 870 214) which ferries by arrangement (cost in 2000 was £2 return per adult, minimum fare £8).

Route	Service	Telephone
Rowardennan / Inverbeg	three services daily in summer	01360 870 273
Inversnaid / Inveruglas	frequent in summer, otherwise phone	01877 386 223
Ardleish / Ardlui	request by hoisting signal at Ardleish; operating hours 0900–1900, April–October	01301 704 243

2.2 Historical background

Much of the Way runs over old military roads built for English soldiers to march along. General George Wade (1673-1748) was an Irishman and Commander-in-Chief of the army in Scotland from 1724-40. His network of 240 miles was vitally important in helping government troops to maintain their grip after the Jacobite risings (see below). The standard width was six feet, with drainage ditches on either side: walking north out of Tyndrum you can clearly see the the cobbled surface.

Wade's legacy is referred to as 'crushing rebellious Scots' in one (never sung) verse of Britain's national anthem. However, most of these roads were actually built by another Irishman, William Caulfeild, who had been Wade's deputy. He was in charge from 1740-67 when four times Wade's mileage was built, including the whole section from Tyndrum to Fort William.

These roads and bridges are still used by hikers 250 years later. Around 450 of Caulfeild's soldiers built and named the Devil's Staircase that climbs out of Glen Coe from Altnafeadh, probably in 1750. The nickname truly belongs to the zig-zagged top section, which cost huge effort to build in such terrain.

The Jacobite risings

In 1688, James VII of Scotland (who was also James II of England) was deposed by popular demand, partly because he was thought to be promoting the Catholic Church. Parliament chose his daughter Mary and her husband William of Orange as joint king and queen (1688-89).

Supporters of the other Stewart line of James VII and his son James (the 'Old Pretender') became known as Jacobites (*Jacobus* is Latin for *James*). Queen Mary showed little interest in Scotland and her Dutch husband was resented. The 1707 Act of Union joining Scotland with England was unpopular, as was the perceived distance from decision-making in London. The Jacobites had widespread popular support, and in 1689-1745, contact was kept up between Scotland and the Jacobite court first in France, then Italy.

Two Jacobite risings took place in 1715 and 1745. The 'Fifteen' focused on the Old Pretender, and the 'Forty-five' on his son, Charles Edward Stewart or 'Bonnie Prince Charlie'. In 1746, the Battle of Culloden marked the final defeat of the Jacobites. However, 'Bonnie Prince Charlie' remained in Scotland for another five months, living in hiding, being pursued all over the highlands and islands by the military.

Rob Roy MacGregor

Rob Roy was born in 1671 into the proscribed MacGregor clan. His fighting strength, long arms and fiery red hair were legendary, and his life was later romanticised in the novels of Sir Walter Scott.

He began as a wealthy man, involved in large-scale cattle droving and dealing around Loch Lomond, with the Duke of Montrose as his patron. His business collapsed after his head drover left taking all his cash. In 1712 the Duke (to whom he owed money) had him bankrupted and outlawed. His house was burned down and family evicted.

Rob Roy swore vengeance, and began a long campaign of thieving cattle, with the occasional kidnap of Montrose's servants. According to legend, he held his prisoners in either his Prison or Cave on Loch Lomondside. The garrison at Inversnaid was built because of Montrose's fear of the MacGregors, who blew it up around 1715 before it was even completed.

He supported the Jacobite side in 1715, but was an onlooker at the Battle of Sherriffmuir. Later he was accused of High Treason and his home burned by troops. He escaped several times, but in 1725 he submitted to General Wade and received the King's pardon. He died in his bed, aged 63.

Caulfeild's military road runs from Tyndrum to Fort William

The Massacre of Glen Coe

In August 1691 King William had ordered all Highland clans chiefs to swear an oath of allegiance before a magistrate by New Year, on pain of death. Old Maclain, chief of the MacDonalds, had delayed to the last moment, finally leaving on 30 December for the wrong destination. Redirected to Inveraray, he was delayed by bad weather and by the Sheriff's absence following New Year celebrations, making him five days overdue.

The government decided that his lateness was reason enough to make an example of the Glen Coe clan by murdering every MacDonald under the age of 70. The murder was planned by senior politicians, and had the authority of King William himself. In February 1692, government troops were billeted upon, and treated hospitably by, the MacDonalds for ten days. Their hosts were not suspicious, believing that the oath had been accepted.

The troops were led by Captain Robert Campbell, a 60-year old alcoholic, gambler and bankrupt. His niece was married to the Maclain's younger son, and he knew nothing of the plan. He opened his orders to find that at 5 am the next morning he had to murder his niece along with the whole family. In all, his soldiers killed around 38 MacDonalds, but at least 300 escaped into the hills, some to die of cold and starvation. Most survived, including Maclain's sons and grandson.

However, public opinion was outraged by the callous abuse of hospitality. The Massacre became a propaganda disaster for William of Orange. An Irishman Charles Leslie wrote a pamphlet about the incident, and in 1695 a commission of inquiry investigated it and issued official reprimands.

Caulfeild's Bridge over the Orchy (built around 1750)

2.3 Munros, Corbetts and Grahams

- A Munro is a Scottish mountain whose summit is over 3000 feet (914 m) in height, provided its peak is not too close to a neighbouring Munro, when it may be classified as merely a 'Top'.

- The Way passes Ben Lomond, the most southerly Munro, and ends near Ben Nevis, the highest. The drop-down maps show more than a dozen other Munros, and a well-prepared hiker can do several as side-trips, weather and time permitting.

- They are named after Sir Hugh Munro, a London-born doctor (1856-1919). His published table (1891) listed 283 such peaks (and 538 Tops). There has been protracted debate about the exact total, and the distinction between a summit and a Top, ever since. The Scottish Mountaineering Club's 1997 figure is 284 Munros and 511 Tops, the revised numbers reflecting more accurate survey methods.

- The first 'Munroist' was the Rev A E Robertson, who completed his final Munro (as then listed) in Glen Coe in 1901 (page 52). Since then, 'Munro-bagging' has become a popular sport, and the list has changed to include the notorious 'Inaccessible Pinnacle' in Skye.

- A few determined individuals manage to climb all the Munros in a single expedition lasting several months, whereas others spread the challenge over a lifetime. At least 100 people become Munroists every year, and as you read this there will be thousands of climbers working on their personal lists.

- A Corbett is smaller: over 2500 feet (762 m) and with a drop of at least 500 feet all round. Several Corbetts are accessible from the Way (see maps).

- A Graham is smaller again: over 2000 feet (610 m), and with a drop of at least 150 metres (492.13 feet) all round. Several Grahams are accessible from the Way (see maps).

Mountain Code

Before you go
Learn the use of map and compass.
Know the weather signs and local forecast.
Plan within your capabilities.
Know simple first aid and the symptoms of exposure.
Know the mountain distress signals.

When you go
Never go alone.
Leave written word of your route, and report on your return.
Take windproofs, waterproofs and survival bag.
Take suitable map and compass, torch and food.
Wear climbing boots.
Keep alert all day.

In winter (November to March)
Each person needs an ice-axe and crampons, and to know how to use them.
The group needs climbing rope, and to know how to use it.
Learn to recognise dangerous snow slopes.
If you need to report an accident on the mountains, telephone 999 and ask for Mountain Rescue.

2.4 Habitats and wildlife

The West Highland Way runs through three main types of habitat:

- river valley and farmland
- woodland
- heath and moorland, described below. For wildlife in and on Loch Lomond, see page 23.

If you are really keen to spot wildlife, carry binoculars and walk alone, or try asking fellow-walkers to remain quiet. If you can set off soon after sunrise, or go out in the evenings, you will find the animals much more active.

River valley and farmland

The valleys of the river Endrick, and its tributary the Blane, support farming and provide rich pasture. Bird life includes oystercatchers and lapwings (commonly known as 'peewit' because of their piercing call), as well as commoner birds such as rooks, gulls and pigeons.

The meandering Endrick has interesting banks, with small sandy cliffs ideal for sand martins, a brownish swallow-like migrant, to dig its deep burrows. Droughts in the Sahel where the bird over-winters have cut its numbers, and the Endrick colonies are important. In the quieter parts of the Endrick, you might even see an otter.

The wetlands at the river mouth are a National Nature Reserve, attracting thousands of over-wintering waders, ducks, geese and whooper swans.

Farmlands support various animals alongside those intended by the farmer. Owls hunt regularly by night, feeding on field mice, voles and shrews. Other predators include kestrels and sparrowhawks, as well as small mammals such as weasels, stoat and foxes. After ploughing and harvesting, the fields leave the prey with nowhere to hide.

Woodland

This includes mixed woodland, semi-natural and commercial plantation, ranging from Mugdock Wood, a Site of Special Scientific Interest, to the semi-natural lochside oakwoods. Oak was planted and harvested from the 18th century on because its bark was needed in the tanning industry. Around Sallochy you will see mature oaks mixed with younger trees such as birch and hazel. The islands also host a mix of trees, including Scots pine, birch and alder.

Kestrel nesting in a spruce tree

Under a 25-year management programme on Loch Lomondside, planted conifers are being felled on large scale and replaced with native broadleaf species. Near Strathcashell Point, the Way skirts the edge of Cashel Forest where Millennium forest planting is under way.

In spring, you will see wildflowers carpeting the woodland floor: bluebells, primroses, wood anemones and wood sorrel are mixed with the lesser celandine (bright yellow star-flowers). Look out for beetles, butterflies, gold-ringed dragonfly and other insects on which birds depend.

The only snake-like animals you might see are the adder and the slow worm – neither a snake nor a worm, but a legless lizard. Adders are poisonous, but normally not dangerous; declining in numbers, they have been a protected species since 1991. Should you meet one (unlikely), leave it alone but watch carefully from a distance. Larger than a slow worm, an adder has an obvious zig-zag pattern and moves quickly.

Slow worm basking in partial sunlight at the Wayside

In woodland, it is often easier to hear birds than to see them: in early summer, listen for the song of cuckoos, wood and willow warblers and chaffinch. You may hear the drumming of the great spotted woodpecker.

Badgers and foxes breed in the heart of the woods, using open land also to find food. The shy pine marten has recently returned to the area. Wildcats are also around, but they are largely nocturnal. You are likely to see feral (semi-wild) goats, especially in the northern lochside, and almost certain to smell their musky droppings.

You may see roe deer in woodland areas anywhere from Mugdock Wood northward: the white kidney shape on the roe deer's rump is distinctive, and they are smaller than their red cousins. Roe deer have never adapted to life without woodland. They were hit hard by the advance of farming and deforestation, and became almost extinct in 18th century England.

Recently, because of the loss of natural predators such as wolf and lynx, deer populations have increased explosively, and the damage they do to tree saplings and bark is threatening their habitat. Careful management is needed to preserve the young trees on which their future depends.

Fallow deer were introduced into the area to adorn the parklands of mansions and castles, and for stalking. They are paler than roe deer and some have distinctive light spots; a few are an amazing pure white. They also occur on some of the islands: fallow deer are particularly good swimmers.

Top left: feral goat
Middle right: red deer stag
Left: wildcat

Heath and moorland

Long stretches of the Way, especially north of Loch Lomond, lie through heather moorland typical of upland Scotland. The ground cover of heather and blaeberry (bilberry) shelters more delicate plants such as milkwort, sundew, butterwort and lousewort.

The moorland's poor, acid peaty soil is perfect for Scots pine. Hardy enough to survive the Ice Age, it used to cover huge areas of Scotland, forming the ancient forest of Caledon.

The golden eagle has a wing-span of 6-7 feet

Look up and you will see many birds of prey. The rabbit population supports a healthy number of buzzards; these are known as 'the tourist's eagle', because visitors so often mistake them for eagles. The golden eagle is much larger, its wing-span nearly double that of the buzzard and its head protrudes more in silhouette.

Smaller birds that thrive in moorland include meadow pipits and skylarks. In summer you may see whinchats and wheatears. If you hear a call like an old-fashioned kettle whistling, look for curlew, with long curved beaks.

On higher ground, such as the Black Mount, watch and listen for grouse (red and black). On really high ground, you might see ptarmigan, camouflaged white in winter, or snow buntings.

On open ground, you may see red deer. In summer, they retreat to the higher ground to escape from pests. In winter they return lower, for better grazing. In the autumn rut, you may see stags fighting or hear them bellowing.

Scots pine is the only pine native to Britain

3.1 From Glasgow to Milngavie

Glasgow is a major European city, a good base for a holiday and worthy of a separate book. It is famous for its architecture, heritage, arts and culture, shopping and friendly inhabitants. Contact the Tourist Information Centre (page 62) for information or buy a good guidebook. This page merely offers practical advice for walkers setting off on the Way.

Glasgow's two stations, Central and Queen Street, are one-third of a mile apart, but a bus shuttles between the two. Trains from the south arrive into Central, whereas trains from the east and north bring you to Queen Street. Most Wayfarers then make a 20-minute train journey to Milngavie (pronounced Mil**guy**). From Glasgow airport the cheapest option is a bus to Buchanan Bus Station (two blocks north of Queen Street) and the quickest is a taxi to Queen Street.

Deeply committed walkers may prefer to walk from the city centre to Milngavie by the Clyde, Kelvin and Allander Walkways (12 miles of linked walkway). Request the free leaflet from the Tourist Information Centre.

From Milngavie railway station, take the underpass under the main road and continue along Station Road into Douglas Street, a busy shopping precinct. You will see the granite obelisk that marks the official start of the Way. Just short of it, look on the right for the waymarker and sign taking you down a path along the stream (the Allander Water).

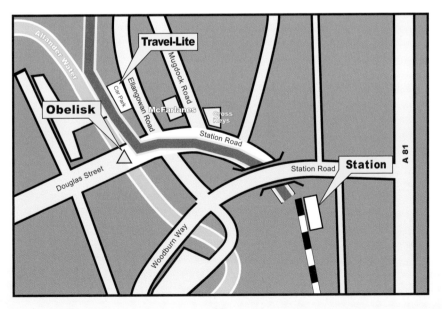

3.2 Milngavie to Drymen

Map	panel 1 (outside back cover)
Distance	12 miles (19 km)
Terrain	starts on tarmac, but mainly tracks and lanes, with some disused railway
Grade	easy walking with no serious gradients; usually good going underfoot
Food and drink	Milngavie, Carbeth Inn, Beech Tree Inn, Drymen
Side-trip	Glengoyne Distillery
Summary	a pleasant, pastoral walk along the valleys of the Blane and Endrick, with good views of the hills

The River Endrick

Milngavie to Drymen step-by-step

- Follow the line of the Allander Water across a road and along a waymarked path which follows, leaves and rejoins the river.

- Shortly the Way turns right, uphill and through some rough moorland with gorse and heather, giving you your first glimpses of the hills beyond.

- At a curved stone wall, notice two curved markers built into the path: they show where Drumclog Moor joins Mugdock Wood. Walk straight on through the woodland, full of wildflowers and birdsong.

- After you leave the Wood at its gates, cross a minor road: turn left onto the road, then immediately right onto the path. This waymarker is sadly sometimes damaged or removed, but look out for the V-shaped self-closing stile, one of many: simply push the posts apart, then let them fall back. Dog-owners need care to get a dog through safely.

- Just after a loch on the right is Carbeth Loch on the left. The countryside feel is now strong, with open views and the strong shape of Dumgoyne: this western outpost of the Campsie Fells is a landmark for miles.

- Turn briefly left onto the B821 then right to continue the Way. However, if seeking refreshment, follow the B821 until it meets the A809, turn left and you will reach the Carbeth Inn shortly, on your left.

- Back on the Way walking north, notice the tree-studded hill of Dumgoyach, a volcanic remnant of pure basalt. Before you reach it, look for the standing stones on high ground to your right (binoculars useful, since they stand on private ground). Carbon-dating reveals them to be late stone age (2600-3100 BC), confirming that the Way was an important through route even in prehistoric times.

Standing stones with Dumgoyne in the background

Milngavie   5   Carbeth   7   Drymen

- The Way curves right around Dumgoyach: turn right after the farm and cross the wooden footbridge over the Blane Water.

- Turn left onto the disused railway track that give you easy walking for the next few miles. This is the trackbed of the Blane Valley Railway, built in 1867 to link Killearn with Glasgow, and later extended to Aberfoyle. Sadly it lasted less than a century.

- Within a mile, you will see on the right the white buildings and pagoda roof of Glengoyne Distillery. If your schedule permits, follow the footpath to take this side-trip (open daily, tel 01360 550 254).

- Shortly after, the Way crosses the A81 at Dumgoyne, a former station now notable for its pub, the Beech Tree Inn. The Way parallels the busy A81 for the next three miles, with traffic noise inevitable. Halfway along this section, the Way passes under a road (the B834).

- Shortly after you re-cross the A81, turn left up a path and onto a minor road through Gartness. Beneath the road bridge the Endrick Water falls over sandstone ledges, sculpting them into strange shapes. After meandering through Drymen, the Endrick deposits its waters and silt in Loch Lomond.

- Continue straight over the cross-roads at the top of the hill, following the minor road all the way until the quarry, where you start to see views of the islands and hills of Loch Lomond.

- The road turns left after the quarry. To continue on the Way, look out for the next waymarker: it is easy to miss the steps leading down and right off the road, just before a small bridge. To reach Drymen itself, however, continue on the minor road for half a mile.

- Note on pronunciation: the 'y' in Drymen is short ('Drimmen'), whereas the 'y' in Tyndrum is long ('Tine-drum'): don't ask why.

3.3 Drymen to Rowardennan

Map	panel 2 (outside back cover)
Distance	15 miles (24 km)
Terrain	mixture of good woodland path, hillside track and rough lochside path
Grade	moderate gradients on Conic Hill (1200 ft), then mainly easy until lochside
Food and drink	Drymen, Balmaha, Rowardennan (hotel)
Side-trip	Inchcailloch (by boat from Balmaha)
Summary	wonderful scenery on the approach to Loch Lomond, especially from Conic Hill, then undulating walking along the wooded lochside

Drymen   Balmaha Rowardennan
          8   7
     Milton   🐕 B837

- From Drymen, retrace your steps along the minor road and turn left down the steps by the bridge.

- Follow the Waymarkers briefly east along the A811 (an old military road) then turn left at Blarnavaid Farm through the stile and along the fence. In spring and summer, the gorse (whin) bushes form an avenue ablaze with yellow.

- Once in the woods, bear left onto a broad track and follow it as it swings around to the left, through the dense 1930s plantation of Garadhban Forest. Cross the roadway (left then immediately right) and continue through the younger, more open plantations, with occasional glimpses of Loch Lomond and the peaks beyond. You will hear, rather than see, the rich variety of bird life, including capercaillie; notice that the trees includes some Scots pine, survivors from the older forest.

- Emerging from the wood, you may have a choice of route. The Way goes up and over Conic Hill but may be closed for lambing (April/May) or because you have a dog (at any time). The bypass avoids these problems, is an easier walk and will be described first. Simply bear left to follow the track downhill; it soon becomes surfaced, then (within a mile) joins the road. Follow the B837 for just over a mile to rejoin the Way at Balmaha's main car park.

- For Conic Hill, bear right to follow the forest track uphill, and over a high stile as you leave the forest. You pass over some moorland, cross a couple of burns (watch out for grouse and, on the streams, dippers). The path now heads straight up the ridge to the obvious summit, a climb of perhaps 500 feet, rewarded by magnificent all-round views.

Conic Hill seen from Loch Lomond

- The Way follows a natural ledge just below the summit, but take the obvious path off to your left for the short steep climb to the very top. Look south west across Loch Lomond to see the line of the Highland Boundary Fault passing through Inchcailloch and other islands. On a clear day you may see Goat Fell, the summit of Arran, some 50 miles away.

Inchcailloch

Visit this island by boat from Balmaha (page 25), arranging your pickup time in advance. This wooded island is rich in wildlife and wildflowers, and has a resident warden in summer.

A simple trail leads to its summit, only 240 feet high but with a terrific view. Its farm and church remnants and burial ground are full of historical interest (page 24).

- Follow the track down the hillside, turning left through the bealach (pass) between two humps. The path heads right, still downhill, through the gate at the edge of conifer woods. Watch for the junction where the Way turns right. You emerge from the woods at Balmaha's main car park, where you can call into the Visitor Centre (page 61).

- Cross the car park and turn right to follow the B road past the bay until it gives out. Turn right up the path up that climbs steeply to Craigie Fort, a rocky outcrop with a superb outlook over the islands.

The view from Conic Hill along the Fault

- After the steep descent, the Way enters the semi-natural oak woodlands so typical of Loch Lomondside. The path varies, sometimes well drained, sometimes undulating and very rough, following the lochside all the way to Rowardennan (seven miles from Balmaha). You hug the shore around Arrochymore point, passing Milarrochy Bay, a popular picnic and boat-launching site, then go through the woods near Stathcashell Point.

- After a short mile along the road, the Way leaves it again at Sallochy, bearing off to the left and broadly following the waterside, with a hilly excursion where the rocks falls sheer into the loch.

Discreet waymarker in Sallochy woods

- After a break in the trees, you cross a footbridge to reach a boathouse. Go round its back and turn up the steep stony path uphill into the plantation of Ross Wood. (Major felling closed this section during parts of 2000, but diversions were clearly signposted.)

- After the descent from Ross Wood, the path returns to the lochside at a shingle beach, from which you may see the submerged crannog offshore. You cross a couple of burns and curve around an inlet, but basically keep heading up the lochside.

- In the final mile or so there is a choice of paths, none of them wrong but all involving a degree of easy scrambling. You glimpse Rowardennan briefly before you reach it over another hill, finally turning left to walk into it along the road.

Looking toward Inchcailloch across Balmaha Bay

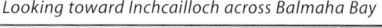

3.4 Rowardennan to Crianlarich

Map	panel 3 (inside back cover)
Distance	20 miles (32 km)
Terrain	mainly rugged walking over lochside rocks and tree roots, some scrambling; last section easier, with final two miles on old military road
Grade	suprisingly strenuous along lochside, care is needed; followed by good paths in Glen Falloch
Food and drink	Rowardennan (hotel), Inversnaid (hotel), Inverarnan, Crianlarich
Side-trip	Ben Lomond
Summary	wild and demanding section, especially north of Inversnaid; fine rapids and falls in Glen Falloch

i

Ben Lomond

As for any Scottish mountain, be prepared for bad weather whatever the season and follow the Mountain Code (page 30). The path is well-worn and normally easy to follow, climbing to 3194 feet virtually from sea level. Although there are several 'false summits' on the way up, the final view from the top is superb. Allow around 4-5 hours for the 8-mile return trip.

Rowardennan to Crianlarich step-by-step

- Time and weather permitting, the ascent of Ben Lomond can be made starting from Rowardennan.

- To continue on the Way, follow the road around the bay, then the track passes the entrance to the youth hostel. The path divides almost at once: bear left along the Way through oak woodlands.

- After a short lochside stretch, the Way crosses a small headland near Ptarmigan Lodge. After 300 yards, you may have a choice of routes for the next three miles: look carefully as the junction is easy to miss. (From time to time this option does not arise for path management reasons.)

- The forest track is higher, easier walking mainly following the contours, but offers limited views in summer because of the foliage. However, after two miles it provides a bench seat with a fine view across to the 'Cobbler', a famous rugged mountain across the loch.

- The lower route start by going down rough steps to the shore, and hugs the shore almost until the two rejoin. The mixture of boulders, tree roots and undulation makes for tough walking, but good practice for the section north of Inversnaid. About halfway there is a huge crag known as Rob Roy's prison (page 27). After another mile, the path heads uphill and slightly inland, past Rowchoish bothy which enjoys splendid views across the loch.

Looking south from the RSPB trail, Inversnaid nestling in the trees

- The routes rejoin, and the path meanders through woodland with some hilly sections. Sometimes you have to pick your own route and occasionally use hands as well as feet.

- Unless you saw a distant glimpse of Inversnaid Hotel, your arrival may feel sudden: you cross two footbridges over the Snaid Burn, just above its attractive Falls. The hotel has a separate walkers' entrance, space for you to leave rucksack and boots, and it makes a good picnic or lunch stop.

- Inversnaid was popular with 19th-century tourists and has many literary associations, for example with Coleridge and the Wordsworths. G M Hopkins wrote about the Snaid Burn in his poem that ends 'Long live the weeds and the wilderness yet.'

- From Inversnaid northward you face the toughest section of the whole Way. There is nothing to daunt a person of normal mobility, but expect progress to be slow. Anyone whose mobility is reduced, or whose feet hurt, can by-pass this section by taking the ferry (page 25) to Inveruglas and catching the bus or walking up the west coast to rejoin the Way at Beinglas Farm.

- Approached in the right frame of mind, with no pressing deadlines, this section is magnificent. It is rugged, remote and rich in plants and wildlife. The path is certainly rough, with many crags, tree-roots and other obstacles, but you feel close to nature and at one with the highlands.

- The Way crosses in front of the hotel, past its boathouse and you now have the option of taking the RSPB trail signposted off to the right. Consider this short detour even if you are not a bird-watcher, as the view from its high point is superb.

- Shortly after the RSPB trail rejoins the Way, the path becomes extremely craggy and after scrambling down a rock-fall you see a sign pointing left for Rob Roy's Cave (page 27). Although not far away, the effort to reach this unimpressive cleft in the rocks is surprising. If rock-hopping does not appeal, you may wish to skip this detour.

Inveruglas — A82 — **Crianlarich**

Rowardennan 7 **Inversnaid** 7 **Inverarnan** 6

- From here onward, you have plenty of scope to make your own Way as the path twists and weaves up and down amongst the hard, old highland rock. Within a couple of miles, however, things get easier and you glimpse 'Island I vow', halfway between Inversnaid and the end of the loch.

- Shortly the loch narrows, and you may hear traffic noise from the busy A82 on the west side. After a small footbridge, the Way bears right and the landscape becomes more grassy and open. After returning to the lochside and another footbridge, the stile tells you that Ardleish is near.

- If your plans include Ardlui, summon the ferry (page 25). Otherwise, follow the Way as it climbs the hillside, and you may catch a first glimpse of three peaks that will dominate the next section: Ben Lui, Ben Oss and Beinn Dubhchraig.

- After climbing a small hill, your view extends over Glen Falloch and the great bend in its river. A short canal used to connect the loch with Inverarnan, so that cattle could be sent to market in Glasgow and beyond.

- Descend the hill to meet the Beinglas Burn. Turn left toward the river, then right to cross the bridge and left to reach Inverarnan. This tiny place offers a choice of hostelries: the historic Drovers' Inn and, opposite, the Stagger Inn.

The Drovers' Inn dates from 1705

- To continue on the Way, cross the footbridge over the Beinglas Burn and enjoy the easier walking in Glen Falloch. You will see gorges, mountain views, rapids and falls; look out for the lovely Falls of Falloch on your left, two miles after Inverarnan.

- More than a mile after the Falls, you pass the white-washed farm of Derrydaroch. Cross the bridge over the river, then turn right onto a gravel path. After a rise and fall, the Way crosses railway and road by a 'sheep creep'.

- Follow the track around to the right, picking up another military road uphill toward a conifer plantation. At the ladder stile, the Way continues left. However, Crianlarich marks your halfway point and is a good place to pause or stay. To reach it, instead turn right down the obvious path to Crianlarich station.

Scots pines in Glen Falloch

The Falls of Falloch

3.5 Crianlarich to Inveroran

Map	**panel 4 (inside back cover)**
Distance	**16 miles (26 km)**
Terrain	**mainly good paths and tracks, much of it along old military road**
Grade	**mainly easy with some moderate ascents and descents (range under 1000 ft)**
Food and drink	**Crianlarich, Tyndrum, Bridge of Orchy, Inveroran (hotel, open February-November)**
Side-trip	**St Fillan's Chapel remains**
Summary	**typical highland walking in glens and over low passes, with many fine mountain views**

West Highland Line train on Beinn Odhar, with Beinn Dorain in the background

Crianlarich to Inveroran step-by-step

- Retrace your steps to pick up the Way west of Crianlarich. The Way forges northwest through trees, grassy slopes and heather. After crossing a burn by footbridge, you climb to reach a broader track, bearing right.

- Shortly, the Way turns left and descends to a railway (the Oban line), passing under a stone viaduct and turning left along the old road. Here the two roads, two railways and river all run along the narrow floor of Strath Fillan. Where the path ends, cross the A82, turning right over the stile to cross the river too.

Gravestones near St Fillan's Chapel

- Walk towards Kirkton Farm but turn left in front of it. On the left, pause to read the information panel about St Fillan's Chapel and its graveyards.

- Keep left, contouring the hillside until you reach Auchtertyre Farm, with its wigwams and campsite. Look up to the right to see the falls on the burn, with the railway viaduct above.

Ben Lui from the River Cononish

Crianlarich 6 Tyndrum 7 Bridge of Orchy 3 Inveroran

- Turn left after the burn and cross the A82 to follow the path alongside the River Cononish (pronounced Cononnish).

- This area is known as Dal Righ ('king's field') in honour of Robert the Bruce, defeated here in 1306. According to legend, he was later inspired by a persistent spider before his famous victory at Bannockburn (1314).

- The Way turns right, following a narrow path to Tyndrum Lower Station. There it curves right to pick up the road into Clifton, an 18th century village created for workers from the lead mines on the upper Cononish. Follow the road to meet the A82, and turn right if visiting the shops and services of Tyndrum.

- From Tyndrum, pick up the road north through Clifton and cross the A82 straight onto an old military road, its surface ideal for rhythmic walking. The views are dominated by two shapely mountains on the right, first Beinn Odhar, then Beinn Dorain.

- After crossing bridges over burn and railway, follow the path up and around the hillside. Shortly you drop down again, passing under the railway and turning right to resume the track northward.

- Look right to see the West Highland Line (which opened in 1894) following the contours (Horseshoe Curve) over viaducts. The Way follows the old military road down to the river, across the stone bridge and left over the stile.

- Walking around the shoulder of Beinn Dorain, notice the mountain views to the north. After a few miles of rugged scenery, you reach the neat little station buildings of Bridge of Orchy.

- Walk under the line and down the minor road toward the A82, which has the Hotel and other services. To continue toward Inveroran, cross the A82 and continue on the narrow A8005 which crosses the river over the famous Bridge of Orchy (page 28).

- After the bridge, bear left off the tarmac up the old road which climbs steadily through pine forest and moorland. At the top, make a short detour up an obvious hillock to the right: this summit, although only 1000 feet, has a superb all-round view.

- The descent is a series of zig-zags, rejoining the A8005 at Inveroran Hotel.

3.6 Inveroran to Kinlochleven

Map	panel 5 (inside back cover)
Distance	18 miles (29 km)
Terrain	mainly good surfaces underfoot but highly exposed; in bad weather this stage must be taken seriously
Grade	moderate climb (to 1000 ft) before Inveroran, then high-level path across Rannoch Moor followed by steep climb out of Glen Coe and long descent into Kinlochleven
Food and drink	Inveroran (hotel), Kingshouse (hotel), Kinlochleven
Side-trip	Glen Coe chairlift and mountaineering museum
Summary	splendid scenery, but even if split into two, this stage is demanding, across the wilds of Rannoch Moor, up the Devil's Staircase and down into Kinlochleven

Loch Tulla and the Black Mount

Inveroran to Kingshouse (10 miles) step-by-step

- The road curves north around the Inveroran Hotel, marking the last signs of civilisation until you reach Kingshouse. You will be crossing Rannoch Moor, one of Britain's largest and wildest moors. This section is extremely exposed: there is simply no shelter. Before you start, ensure you are well provisioned and equipped to face poor weather. Do not stray from the path, as in places you could sink into the peat bog.

- From Victoria Bridge, you have a good view of Loch Tulla, with its crannog. From here, the Way follows an old drover's route, while the old military road climbs higher, to the left. After a steady climb alongside the plantation, the two rejoin at a reedy lochan shortly before Ba Bridge.

- From Ba Bridge, look along the River Ba, which here runs through a tiny gorge of red granite slabs. Three miles to the west you will see Coireach a' Ba, said to be Scotland's largest corrie (circular hollow). This whole area is known as the Black Mount, though it is more plateau than mountain.

- A mile further along, you reach the ruins of Ba Cottage and start to climb more steeply. Within a further mile you reach the summit, around 1500 feet, and begin the long descent to Kingshouse.

- The views start to feature the mountain photographed on the front cover: Buachaille Etive Mor, the 'great herdsman' guarding the junction of two glens, Etive and Coe. Its steep faces are paradise for rock climbers, but it can also be summited by competent hill walkers.

- Shortly look for the chairlift of the Glencoe Ski Centre up to your left. If you have time for the side-trip, turn left at Blackrock Cottage. Otherwise turn right, cross the A82 carefully and continue to the Kingshouse Hotel.

> *i*
> **Glencoe Ski Centre (Tel 01855 851 226)**
>
> *Chairlift (daily in summer) rises to 2400 feet in 15 minutes, giving superb views. Licensed restaurant. Museum of Scottish Ski-ing and Mountaineering houses belongings of A E Robertson (page 29), who climbed his last Munro in Glen Coe.*

- The Kingshouse has been an inn since 1800, and has a long history associated with salt-smuggling and cattle-droving. Its location is both romantic and desolate, encircled by mountains and at the head of Glen Coe, on which the 1692 Massacre has cast an indelible shadow (page 28).

- If staying at the Hotel or free campsite nearby, walk out in the early morning to see the deer that come down from the hills to feed on left-overs. If you are heading on to Kinlochleven, this makes a good refreshment and rest stop.

Kingshouse to Kinlochleven (8 miles) step-by-step

- Cross the river behind the hotel and walk up the minor road until the fence, where you turn left and walk straight for half a mile. Before reaching the A82, turn right over a stile and follow the path uphill.

- If you prefer the alternative route (more affected by the main road and wetter underfoot), ignore the stile, cross the A82 carefully and pick your way alongside the River Coupall (see map panel 5).

- The two routes converge at Altnafeadh, where the Way starts its stiff climb out of Glen Coe up the military road known as the 'Devil's Staircase' (page 26). Many people find the name intimidating, but the surface is good and the gradient limited by zig-zags of increasing size. The summit is less than 850 feet above Altnafeadh, and is marked by a cairn (pile of stones).

Inveroran — 10 — Kingshouse — 3 — Altnafeadh — 5 — Kinlochleven

- Pause to savour the mountains of Glen Coe behind you, before walking on to the saddle between two 2000+ foot mountains. As you continue north, a new vista opens up, with the ridges and peaks of the Mamores backed by the hunched massif of Ben Nevis, contrasting with the conical Carn Mor Dearg to its right.

- Once past the shoulder of the hill, look to your right for views of the Blackwater Reservoir. The dam is half a mile long and 30 yards high, and was built between 1905 and 1909. It was built by human muscle power (3000 navvies or labourers), using an overhead rope railway in place of roads, and was at the time Britain's largest hydro-electric power scheme.

- As you descend, you will see the penstock (head of the pipeline) from where the pipes carry water down a 1 in 4 gradient for over half a mile. Indeed you may regret that the Way takes a less direct route than the water: the descent into Kinlochleven takes a surprisingly long time. With good eyesight or binoculars, you may see the line of the Way running west under the Mamores.

- The Way follows the pipes to the back of the aluminium works, then crosses them and turns up a road bridging the River Leven. It then turns left and follows the military road alongside a housing scheme.

- The Way turns left at Morrison Crescent along a riverside path and soon meets the B863. There you turn left (back across the river) to reach the centre of Kinlochleven, or right to continue along the Way.

- Kinlochleven was a creation of the 20th century. It began as a few small crofts and a hunting lodge, but expanded hugely with the building of the British Aluminium Company works. Kinlochleven's aluminium was of unique purity, but it could not compete on price with the huge plants elsewhere, nor keep pace with worldwide demand from the motor and aircraft industries.

- Although the works closed in June 2000, the old Alcan buildings were being converted into bunkhouses and climbing walls, supporting Kinlochleven's development as a walking centre. Kinlochleven's unusual story is told in the Visitor Centre (see page 56), where you can also buy the fascinating book *Children of the Dead End* by Patrick MacGill.

3.7 Kinlochleven to Fort William

Map	panel 6 (page 64)
Distance	14 miles (23 km)
Terrain	first half old military road, then rough paths in Nevis Forest, finally some tarmac into Fort William
Grade	steep climb out of Kinlochleven, then no serious gradients until Nevis Forest (up to 900 ft), finally descending into Fort William
Food and drink	none between Kinlochleven and Fort William
Side-trip	The Aluminium Story
Summary	begins as mainly open upland walking, with views toward Ben Nevis; after the splendour of Glen Nevis, the Way finishes on tarmac in Fort William

Grey Mare's Tail, Kinlochleven

Kinlochleven to Fort William step-by-step

- From your accommodation, pick up the waymarkers which follow the north side of the River Leven. For the Grey Mare's Tail waterfall detour, follow signs off to the right before you leave Kinlochmore (half-mile round trip).

- The Way now bears right on a track through the woods, following the route of the old military road for seven miles. It isn't always obviously a road, but look out for stones set into stream beds and flights of rough stone steps. At first you climb steeply, with zig-zags to ease the gradient, then more gently.

The Aluminium Story
Tel 01855 831 663

Open weekdays in summer (at least 10 am to 6 pm) also October-March for 4 hours (Tuesdays and Thursdays)

Unusual visitor centre clad in aluminium, attached to the library in Linnhe Road. It explains how the hydro-electric scheme was created, and the role of aluminium production in Kinlochleven.

Audiovisual displays and video presentation; giant sundial and seating outside.

- You see glimpses of Loch Leven in the odd clearing. Then after a hairpin bend you emerge from the birchwood to a splendid view of the loch framed by mountains to its south, including the shapely Pap of Glencoe.

- After a total ascent of perhaps 900 feet you reach the Lairigmor, the 'great pass', a broad glen passing between the high hills to your left and the even higher Mamores to your right. The walking is easy, the gradients gentle, sheep roam freely and you will see disused and ruined farm buildings from the days where hill farmers lived here.

- After a while, the Way (and the whole glen) swings north and just before you enter woodland it passes old shielings (temporary shelter for crofters' families minding the cattle). At the edge of this wood is a seat and a view of Lochan Lunn Da-Bhra (pronounced Lund**av**ra), home to a mythical bull said to lure and drown crofters' cattle. You are roughly half-way, and this may be a good time to seek a picnic spot.

- The information shelter marks where the Way leaves the military road, which you have been following ever since Glen Falloch. (Anyone who needs a shortcut should keep straight along this road to reach Fort

William within 4½ miles of tarmac.) To keep to the Way, however, bear right through the woods, leaving them shortly over a high stile and head for Glen Nevis (two miles longer).

- The final stretch consists of rough walking through forestry plantations, with occasional open breaks giving views northward toward the huge bulk of Ben Nevis. In just under three miles, look on your right for the hill of Dun Deardail which has an Iron Age fort.

- For a closer look, follow the path which starts at the fence and leads right to the hilltop. The rubble walls are now largely grassed over, but they were vitrified, ie melted into a glassy mass, by fire. Vitrified forts are widespread in Britain, mainly dating from 100 BC to 100 AD: archaeologists think the fire was caused by attackers burning timber cross-pieces that strengthened the fort.

- Shortly after the fort, you descend into Glen Nevis, picking up a broad, bending forest road. After a mile, a spur bends sharply back to the right, leading to Glen Nevis Youth Hostel. The Way continues northward on the forest road, and after 700 yards turns sharp right steeply downhill, then forks left down past a small cemetery. Go through the wooden gate and turn left at the narrow public road along the River Nevis.

- Follow the roadside pavement for 1½ miles to reach your destination, passing a massive boulder on your left, called Clach Comhairle (the stone of counsel). According to legend, this dispenses wise advice one night a year while magically turning around three times. From the obelisk at Nevis Bridge, head straight on for the centre of Fort William and the railway station (half a mile).

Kinlochleven   **Fort William**

14

3.8 Fort William and Ben Nevis

Originally Fort William was called Inverlochy, its crude fort built in 1654-5 by General Monk. This was replaced by a stone fort in 1690, when the town was renamed after William III (William of Orange). The town is a centre for tourism and shopping and a popular base for hikers and climbers.

- Although the Fort withstood many conflicts, in 1890 the railway was built over it, and little has survived. Look for traces opposite the railway station and supermarket car park, on the banks of Loch Lochy.

- Glen Nevis is an area of outstanding beauty for hikers, with waterfalls, the precarious three-string bridge and a wealth of wild flowers and birds. Its Visitor Centre is open daily from Easter to end October (tel 01397 705 922).

- The town's West Highland Museum has information about the town and its fortifications: open year-round Monday to Saturday, also on Sunday afternoons in July/August (tel 01397 702 169).

- Take a boat trip from the Town Pier to Seal Island for a really close approach to seals. If possible, go when the tide is low, to see more seals: sailings daily April-October (tel 01397 703 919).

- Climb Cow Hill (942 ft) for splendid views over mountains and lochs. You may see the line of the River Lochy and the Caledonian Canal leading up the Great Glen.

- Two miles northeast of the town on the A82, the Ben Nevis distillery has a visitor centre, offers tours and tastings, and is open Monday to Saturday, Easter to October (tel 01397 700 200).

- At Corpach, on the A830, visit Treasures of the Earth, one of Europe's finest collections of gemstones and crystals, displayed in caves and mining scenes: open daily (tel 01397 772 283).

Ben Nevis

Climbing Ben Nevis by the normal route makes a grand finale to walking the Way. It is a strenuous walk rather than a technical climb, but must be taken seriously. To call the normal ascent 'the tourist route' is highly misleading: the Mountain Rescue Service is called out too often by ill-prepared tourists.

In summer months, if you prepare sensibly and are prepared to turn back if conditions change, the Ben need not be dangerous. Collect the free leaflet *Walking the Ben Path* from the Visitor Centre, and get a local weather forecast. Read and follow the Mountain Code (page 30). If you don't know how to use a compass, go with someone who does, and take a large-scale map anyway. Bear in mind the following:

- More than 157 inches of rain and snow falls on the summit each year. The mean annual temperature is below freezing-point, and there are, on average, 261 gales per year.

- Start from the beginning of the old pony track at Achintee, on the east bank of the River Nevis, or from the Glen Nevis Youth Hostel. Allow 3 to 5 hours for the ascent and 1½ to 2½ for descent.

- Ben Nevis and most of Glen Nevis have been designated a Site of Special Scientific Interest, because of the range of geological features, and plant and animal life. Pressure of numbers has badly eroded the zig-zag path: it is vital that you keep to the path, confining this erosion, and reducing the disturbance to wildlife such as ground-nesting birds.

- On the upper slopes of the Ben, look out for snow buntings and ptarmigan (speckled in summer, white in winter).

- Finally, here is a humbling fact: in the annual race (held on the first Saturday in September) the record for the return journey to the summit from Fort William stands at around 85 minutes.

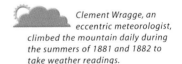

Clement Wragge, an eccentric meteorologist, climbed the mountain daily during the summers of 1881 and 1882 to take weather readings.

Later, a weather observatory worked from 1883-1904. Its bridle-path was built to allow ponies to service the observatory. This path is now the normal ascent route.

Cliffs on the Ben's summit drop 2000 feet

Sadly, people still die on the Ben, caught by worsening weather and confusion on the summit cliffs. If you have any doubts by the halfway point (Red Burn Ford), turn back. In bad weather, the only safe escape route is to walk from the trig pillar 150 yards along a grid bearing of 231°, then follow 282° to clear the plateau. Unless you are competent with a compass, and can correct magnetic bearings, don't risk it.

Ben Nevis at dusk, seen from the west

Reference

Contact details

All phone numbers are shown as dialled from within the UK. From another country, dial the access code then 44 followed by the number below minus its leading zero. NB This list was checked prior to publication, but phone numbers and website addresses are liable to change without notice.

Service providers

Easyways (Julie Deans, accommodation booking)
01324 714 132   info@easyways.com

Transcotland (Andrew Pointer, self-guided holidays)
01887 820 848   info@transcotland.com

Travel-Lite (baggage handling, mid-April to mid-September)
0141 956 7890   info@travel-lite-uk.com

Transport

Scottish Citylink (Scottish buses)
08705 505 050   www.citylink.co.uk

National Express (national buses)
0990 808 080   www.gobycoach.com

Railtrack (national rail)
08457 484 950   www.railtrack.co.uk

Scotrail (Scottish rail)
0345 484 950   www.scotrail.co.uk

Edinburgh Airport
0131 333 1000

Glasgow Airport
0141 887 1111

easyJet
0870 6000 000   www.easyJet.com

Weather information

Weathercall (local 7-day forecast)
09068 500 424

Glasgow Weather Centre
0141 248 3451

Scottish Avalanche Information Service
0800 0960 007   www.sais.gov.uk

Route Management, official websiteand Visitor Centres

The official West Highland Way website is well worth visiting for information on accommodation, updates and events:

www.west-highland-way.co.uk

If you want the printed leaflet in addition, send a stamped addressed envelop (SAE) to:

The West Highland Way Ranger
Balloch Castle
Balloch
G83 8LX
Tel 01389 758 216
Fax 01389 755 721

You can also request the official leaflet, or provide feedback on the Way, by email to

info@west-highland-way.co.uk

There are visitor centres at Balmaha (open daily Easter - October, tel 01360 870 470) and at Glen Nevis (open daily year-round, tel 01397 705 922). Visit them for their information displays and publications, or to contact the Ranger Service.

West Highland Wayfarer

This informative broadsheet is available free from outlets along the Way or direct from its publisher: send SAE to

Famedram Publishers Ltd
Mill Business Centre
P O Box 3
Ellon
AB41 9EA

The Scottish Rights of Way and Access Society

This publishes a newsletter, campaigns for rights of access and distributes many useful publications:

24 Annandale Street
Edinburgh
EH7 4AN
Tel 0131 558 1222

Scottish Youth Hostels

This registered charity distributes information about its hostels; booking is recommended. Membership (as of 2000) cost £6 pa but you can join on your first stay at a hostel, or pay a non-member supplement of £1 per night; no upper age limit, sheet sleeping bag provided, prices range from £7-£13 per night.

7 Glebe Crescent
Stirling
FK8 2JA
Tel 01786 891 400

email   activities@syha.org.co
website   www.syha.org.uk

Tourist Information Centres

The Way is covered by the Glasgow and Clyde Valley Tourist Board (Milngavie to Drymen), AILLST (Drymen to Bridge of Orchy) and the Fort William and Lochaber Tourist Board (Rannoch Moor to Fort William). Between them, they operate Tourist Information Centres:

Greater Glasgow Tourist Board
0141 204 4400
Drymen TIC
01360 660 068 (May to September only)
Tyndrum TIC
01838 400 246 (April to October only)
Fort William TIC
01397 703 781 (open year-round)

Maps

The West Highland Way area is covered by sheets 64, 57, 56, 50 and 41 of the Ordnance Survey Landranger Series (1:50,000) and in more detail, over 13 sheets, by their Pathfinder Series (1:25,000). The OS 'Outdoor Leisure 39' is a detailed (1:25,000) map of Loch Lomond that also shows the Way from Milngavie to Inverarnan. Harvey's Map Services publishes the official West Highland Way map (1:40,000), and other relevant maps: for example, their Glen Coe and Ben Nevis Superwalkers (1:25,000).

The maps in this book are 1:100,000 and were specially created by Cartographic Consultants of Edinburgh.

Acknowledgements

The publisher wishes to thank the following for commenting on parts of the manuscript in draft: Steve Westwood (Path Manager), Steve Nunn, Don Coombs, Julie Deans, Mary McCallum, Gilbert McVean and Lindsay Megarry. Their efforts resulted in many improvements, but we accept responsibility for any flaws. We welcome comments from readers, preferably by email to info@rucsacs.com.

Photo credits

Ken Paterson/Still Moving Picture Co (front cover); Jacquetta Megarry (32 images), Argyll, the Isles, Loch Lomond, Stirling & Trossachs Tourist Board (AILLST, 13 images), Celia Burn, David Paterson, Gordon Riddle, Jim Strachan.

Index

A

accommodation 6, 11, 61, 62
adders 32
Aluminium Story 56

B

baggage, weight and handling 12, 14
Balmaha 41, 61
Ben Lomond 43
Ben Nevis 59-60
blisters, prevention and treatment 14, 18
boots, advice on buying 15
Bridge of Orchy 28, 50

C

camping 11, 19
care with livestock 10
cashels 24
Caulfeild, Major William 26
checklist, for packing 18
clothing, advice on choosing 16
Conic Hill 40
conversion (miles/km, feet/m) 20
Corbetts 29
Country Code 10
crannogs 24
Crianlarich 45, 48

D

distances and time needed 6, 7, 13
deer, red, roe and fallow 33-34, 53
Devil's Staircase 26, 53
dogs 10, 40
Drymen 38, 41
Dumgoyach standing stones 37

E

Endrick, River 23, 31, 36, 38
equipment/gear 15-18

F

Falloch, Falls of 47
ferries, Loch Lomond 25
Fort William 55, 58-60

G

Glasgow 37
Glen Coe and Massacre 28, 52-4
Glengoyne Distillery 38
Glen Nevis 11, 57-8, 61
goats, feral 33
Grahams 29

H

habitats and wildlife 31-4
Highland Boundary Fault 22, 41
historical background 26-8

I

Inchcailloch 21, 24, 41
Inverarnan 46
Inveroran 48, 51
Inversnaid 27, 45

J

Jacobite risings 26

K

Kingshouse 52-53
Kinlochleven 51, 55

L

livestock, care with 10
Loch Lomond 21-5
Long Distance Routes in Scotland 4

M

mileage, daily 13
military roads 26, 40, 52-4, 56
Milngavie 35
mobile phones 20
Mountain Code 30
Mugdock Wood 32
Munros, Sir Hugh Munro 9, 29

N

non-walking activities 9

P

packing checklist 18
pests (midges and clegs) 9, 18
planning your travel 7-8
poles 16
powan 23
preparation for walking 14-18
public transport 61

R

Rob Roy MacGregor 27
Rowardennan 42, 45
rucksacks, advice on buying 16

S

Scots (Caledonian) pine 34
season, best for walking 9
slow worms 32

T

Tourist Information Centres 62
transport and travel 7-8, 61
Tyndrum 50

W

Wade, General 26, 27
water, carriers for drinking 17
weather 5, 61
wildcats 33
wildlife and habitats 31-4

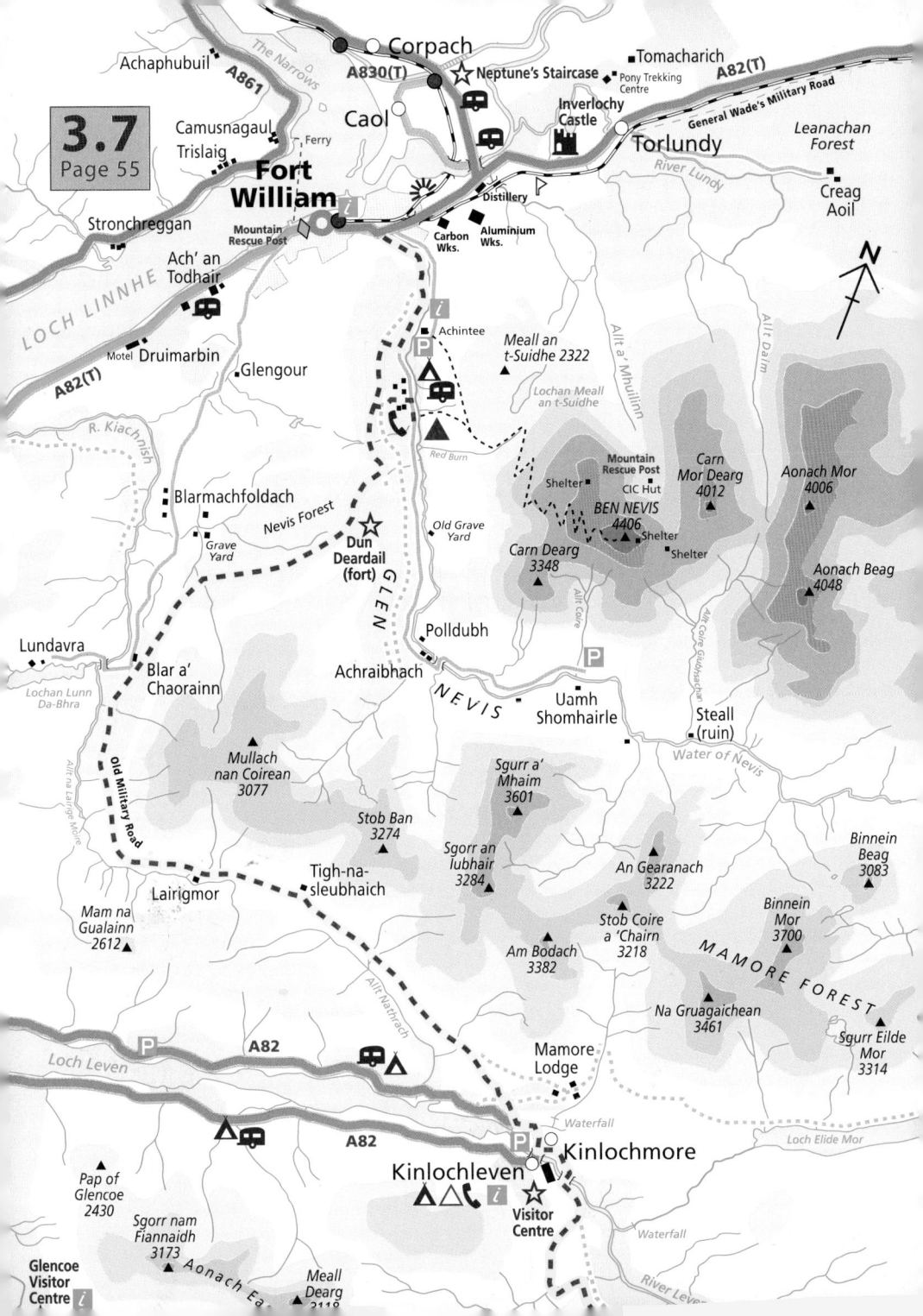